MUHAMMAD ALI

Jane Rollason

LEVEL 2

SCHOLASTIC

Author: Jane Rollason

Publisher: Jacquie Bloese

Editor: Mary Gallagher

Designer: Mo Choy

Picture research: Amparo Escobedo

Photo credits:

Cover: S.Weston/Getty Images

Pages 4 & 5: S. Weston, C. Smith/Popperfoto, J. Peodincuk/NY Daily News Archive, Library of Congress/Corbis/, Hulton Archive, Michel Ochs Archives, S. Weston, H Benson/xpres, PL Gould, R. Platzer, D. J. Hogan/Getty Images; BardoczPeter/iStock

Page 6: P. L. Photo and Video/ShutterStock

Page 8: USA TODAY Network/SIPA USA/PA

Page 13: M. E. Newman/Sport Illustrated/Getty Images

Page 15: C. Smith/Popperfoto/Getty Images

Page 16: L. Trievnor/Express/ Getty Images

Page 19: Keystone/Getty Images

Page 21: S. Weston/Getty Images

Page 23: J. Peodincuk/NY Daily News Archive/ Getty Images

Pages 24 & 25: Central Press, D. Fenton, Hulton Archive/Getty Images

Page 27: Bettmann/Getty Images

Page 30: R. Abbott Sengstacke/Getty Images

Pages 32 & 33: P. Christain/Getty Images

Pages 36 & 37: Bettmann/Getty Images

Page 39: PA Archive/PA

Pages 42 & 43: T. Tanuma/Sports Illustrated/Getty Images; F. Tewkesbury/Evening Standard/Getty Images

Page 45: S. Schapiro/Corbis/Getty Images

Page 47: A. Roque/AFP/Getty Images

Pages 48 & 49: M. Cooper/Getty Images, J. Watson/AFP/Getty Images

Pages 50 & 41: OSTILL/iStock, C. Petersen; E. Mulholland/Getty Images

© Scholastic Ltd., 2017

Mary Glasgow Magazines (Scholastic Ltd.)
Euston House
24 Eversholt Street
London NW1 IDB

Printed in Malaysia

Contents

MUHAMMAD ALI 1942–2016

Muhammad Ali was the world's greatest boxer. But he didn't just fight inside the boxing ring. He fought outside the ring too, for better lives for black people.

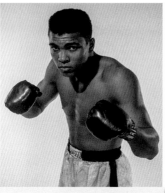

Cassius moved to Miami, Florida, in 1962 to train with Angelo Dundee. They worked together for 21 years.

Born in 1942, Cassius Clay lived in Louisville, Kentucky, until he was 20 years old.

After Cassius met Malcolm X, he changed his name to Muhammad Ali.

PLACES

Louisville, Kentucky was Muhammad Ali's home before he moved to Miami in Florida.

Louisville, 1960s

THE BOXERS

Ali fought the best boxers in the world. He beat them all.

George Foreman

Joe Frazier

Sonny Liston

Henry Cooper

ALI'S WIVES

Ali had four wives and nine children.

Sonji Roi

Belinda Boyd

Veronica Porsche

Lonnie Williams

BOXING WORDS

boxer

crowd

referee

corner

gloves

canvas

ropes

MUHAMMAD ALI

PROLOGUE

A shiny red and white bike stood outside the front door of a four-room house in Louisville, Kentucky. It was a twelfth birthday present, and it belonged to Cassius Clay. His parents worked hard to find the sixty dollars to buy it for him. He rode it happily around his hometown until one day, someone took it.

Cassius was angry and upset. He found a police officer and told him about his bike.

'I'm gonna* fight the guy who took my bike,' Cassius said.

The officer smiled.

'Do you know how to fight?' he asked.

'No, but so what?' said Cassius angrily. 'I'll fight him anyway.'

'Maybe you should learn how to fight first,' he laughed.

'Where can I learn?' asked Cassius.

'In my boxing club,' said the officer.

The white police officer was called Joe Martin, and he ran a boxing club after school. Cassius joined and Joe became his first trainer.

Cassius didn't get his bike back, but he was now on the way to being the world's greatest boxer.

* gonna = 'going to' in informal English

CHAPTER 1
Tomorrow's champion

Muhammad Ali was born on 17th January, 1942, and his parents named him Cassius Clay Jr. He had one younger brother, named Rudolph. Their mother, Odessa Clay, worked hard to send her two boys to school and buy clothes for them. Cassius Clay Sr*, their father, worked hard too. He also liked to drink and was often in trouble, but it was a happy home. Cassius Sr played music and wrote songs, and Cassius Jr was always laughing and playing tricks on everyone. The Clays were a Christian family, and Odessa took her two boys to church every Sunday. The Clay house in Louisville was in a part of town where only black people lived. Louisville, Kentucky was a safe town for Cassius and his brother if they stayed in the black areas.

Cassius, right, and younger brother, Rudolph.

* Sr = Senior; in America, parents often give their first son the same name as the father. They call the father Sr (Senior) and the son Jr (Junior).

The family name of Clay was a slave name. Slaves in the 1800s took the name of their owner, and many kept these names after they became free. Odessa Clay also came from a slave family. Her great grandmother* was a slave called Dinah and her great grandfather was a white man.

Kentucky is a state in the south-east of the USA. When black slavery ended in 1865 in the United States, ideas in the South did not change. Most southern white people did not want to live with black people. So the South made new laws. Blacks and whites had different buses, schools, shops, churches and workplaces. This was 'segregation', and the laws were the 'Jim Crow laws'. One hot day when he was a child, Cassius went into a shop for white people. He wanted a drink of water, but they wouldn't give him one because he was black. He was too young to understand, but he knew it was wrong.

In 1955, just a year after Cassius started learning to box with Joe Martin, a fourteen-year-old black boy was in the news. His name was Emmet Till, and he was from Chicago in the North, where there was no segregation. Emmet was staying with his cousin's family in Mississippi in the South. He and his cousin were in town one day, and Emmet was joking around. He called out to a pretty white woman. A black boy could not speak to a white woman like this, but Emmet didn't know that. When Emmet saw his cousin's face, he knew he was in trouble. That night, the woman's husband and brother pulled Emmet from his bed in his uncle's home. They hurt him very badly and then they killed him. When Emmet's mother came to collect her son's body, he didn't look like her son anymore. The white men did not go to prison.

* great grandmother = your grandmother's mother

9

Photographs of Emmet appeared in *Jet*, a magazine for African-Americans. Cassius Sr showed the pictures to his sons and told them the story. Cassius was upset and scared. Until then, he felt safe as a black boy in a black part of town. But he was nearly fourteen, like Emmet. He loved joking around, like Emmet. He saw that the law was on the side of white people and against black people.

* * *

Boys from Joe Martin's boxing club travelled all over the South for fights at the weekends. Joe Martin's wife drove them. When they stopped to eat along the way, the restaurants often had 'Whites Only' signs on the door. Mrs Martin would buy hamburgers for all the boys, and they would eat them in the car. The boys had to use 'Coloreds*' toilets, and could not go in the 'Whites' toilets.

Working harder than the other boys, Cassius learned quickly with Joe. He was soon winning boxing titles and he started to have his own fighting style. He danced around the ring, he was very quick with his hands and he could punch hard. Because he grew very tall and had long arms, other boxers couldn't reach him. He felt at home in the boxing ring, and he wanted to be great. His day often started at four o'clock in the morning, with a run through the streets of Louisville. At first, the local police would stop him. Soon they weren't surprised to see him, and they left him alone.

Joe Martin also ran a local TV show called *Tomorrow's Champions*. His young boxers appeared on the show on Friday nights. Just six weeks after he joined the club, Cassius had his first fight in the ring. He won his fight and he was on the show. 'Did you see me on TV?' he asked

* 'Coloreds' described non-white people in the segregation areas, especially African-Americans.

everyone at school on Monday. 'One day, I'm going to be Heavyweight Champion of the World.'

Cassius and Joe worked together for six years until Cassius was eighteen. In that time, Cassius won 100 fights and lost only one.

Boxing was Cassius's life in his teenage years. When he left Central High School in 1960 aged eighteen, he could only just read and write. He didn't do well in his last exams, and he came 376th out of the 391 students who left school that year. But he wasn't interested in results. He had a very different goal. 'I'm going to be an Olympic champion this summer,' he told everyone at Central High.

Cassius had a place on the U.S. Olympic team. The 1960 Olympics were in Rome, and he nearly didn't go because he was frightened of flying.

'I'm not going,' he said to Joe.

'If you want to be a great fighter,' Joe said, 'you have to win the Olympic title.'

Finally, Cassius agreed to go.

The Olympic team went first to New York, where the young boxers visited Harlem, New York's black area. It was not like sleepy Louisville. The city streets were busy and full of people in fashionable clothes. On many of the street corners, there were men standing on boxes. They were shouting their ideas to people as they walked by. Cassius stopped to listen to one man.

'Buy black,' the man shouted. 'Buy from black businesses and shops. Don't get your food from white folks*.'

His message wasn't dangerous, but nobody talked like that in Louisville.

'Can he say that in the street?' Cassius asked a sports

* folks = 'people' in U.S. informal English

writer who was with them.

'Yeah,' said the writer. 'This is the North.'

Cassius walked around this new world, looking at everything with wide open eyes. They stopped outside Sugar Ray's, a famous Harlem restaurant and bar. Boxing champion Sugar Ray Robinson owned it. At that time, many sports writers believed Sugar Ray was the world's greatest boxer. He was good-looking too, and for Cassius, a hero. Sugar Ray drove up to his club in a pink Cadillac and said hi to the young boxers.

'Some day I'm gonna have two Cadillacs,' said Cassius that evening, 'one to ride around in and one to look at.'

The boxing team moved on from the world of black Harlem to the Olympic village in Rome. Here was the whole world in one place. Cassius talked to everyone, even when they didn't speak the same language. He learned everyone's name and he was very popular in the village. The crowds at his fights loved him too, with his new and exciting style. Cassius defeated the European champion, Ziggy Pietrzykowski from Poland, to win the Olympic title.

'I'm young. I'm good-looking. I'm fast. I'm pretty. And I always win!' he said. He wore his Olympic medal for days after the fight, even in bed. He was happy to be an American.

'The United States is the best country in the world, including yours,' he said to a Soviet* sports writer.

'What about the way blacks have to live in the South?' asked the writer.

'We've got good people working on that,' Cassius answered.

* The modern country of Russia was called the Soviet Union (USSR) at this time.

Back home in America, Cassius was becoming famous, and he loved it. He wanted everyone to know him and talk about him. He wanted to be right at the centre of everything.

There was a hero's welcome for the Olympic champion back in his hometown of Louisville. All the important men of the city met Cassius, and he rode around town in an open-top car. For a short time, nobody saw his colour. He went back to Central High School and showed the school his beautiful, shiny medal. Nobody remembered his exam results now.

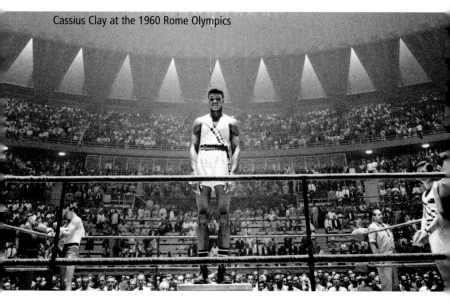
Cassius Clay at the 1960 Rome Olympics

Kentucky still had the Jim Crow laws, and segregated life went on. Even with his Olympic medal, Cassius couldn't use the seats on a Louisville bus. Cassius was always smiling and joking. But some big questions were going around in his head. He was starting to look for answers.

CHAPTER 2
'As fast as lightning'

Cassius Clay was Olympic champion and nobody could defeat him. He was also good-looking and funny. The boxing world was very interested in him, but boxing was a dark business at that time. A lot of bad people made a lot of money, and the fighters often had nothing when they retired.

A group of local Louisville millionaires got together and decided to help Cassius. They wanted to look after their local boy. Of course, they were hoping to make some money too.

They wanted to be fair to Cassius and they offered him good money to fight for them. He liked the offer and he signed with the Louisville group for four years.

'Is there anything you would like?' they asked, as he put the pen down.

'I'd like a Cadillac,' Cassius said.

'Sure,' they said, and sent him to choose a car. Of course, Cassius chose a pink Cadillac. He drove around town feeling like Sugar Ray Robinson.

Just three days later, Cassius's first fight for the new Louisville team took place. The young boxer was worried. Opposite him in the ring was Tunney Hunsaker, a thirty-year-old white police officer. His fighting style was new to Cassius. But Cassius didn't need to worry. Tunney tried every boxing trick to upset Cassius, but none of them worked. Cassius won in six rounds.

'He was as fast as lightning,' said Tunney, 'and just too good for me.' The two men became friends, and Ali later remembered that Tunney's punch was one of the hardest.

Cassius had money now. He bought a bigger house for

his parents, moving them to a better part of town. The Louisville millionaires decided he needed a better trainer than Joe Martin, but there was no one in Louisville. They chose the 5th Street Gym in Miami, Florida. A trainer called Angelo Dundee ran the gym, and he was the best in the business. Before Cassius left for Florida, he gave his pink Cadillac to his mother.

Cassius working with trainer Angelo Dundee.

Cassius loved Miami. He loved the sunshine and the new life. He loved Angelo Dundee, and he loved the 5th Street Gym. It was upstairs in an old building, above a shop. The floors weren't very safe, and Angelo was worried that his boxers would fall right through to the shop below. The gym was always hot and noisy, and full of fighters, including many Cuban fighters. Many Cubans left Cuba at this time because of Fidel Castro*, and

* Castro led a Communist government in Cuba, a country near the USA.

came to live in Miami. Cassius loved to watch the Cuban fighters. They moved quickly and had different styles of punching. Cassius watched and learned, and he worked and trained. He changed from a good young fighter into a brilliant boxer. He danced around his opponents and they couldn't catch him with their punches. He waited until they were tired, and then he punched hard.

Cassius before his fight with Henry Cooper in London

As well as being a new kind of boxer, Cassius was a new kind of showman. He loved people to watch him and listen to him. He was funny and quick, and always had a lot to say. Before each fight, Cassius chose the round when his opponent would lose. He was almost always right.

He was a joker in the ring. He loved playing with words, and made jokes about his opponents. He talked all the time so his opponent became angry. When someone was angry, Cassius believed, they stopped thinking clearly.

* * *

After two years in Miami, Angelo Dundee took Cassius to London, the home of boxing. The modern sport started there in 1867 when the Marquess of Queensberry decided on new boxing laws. On this first trip, Londoners didn't know who Cassius Clay was. They soon learned. Cassius went out on the streets with some British police officers in their famous hats. He trained in Hyde Park. He walked around London's fashionable streets in his expensive clothes, with a beautiful coat on. In the 1960s, London life was cool and exciting. The new young boxer, Cassius Clay, was cool and exciting too.

Britain's best boxer at that time was Henry Cooper, and the fight between Clay and Cooper took place at Wembley Stadium. 'Cassius will win,' people said. Cassius agreed with them.

'This is no jive*, he'll go in Round five,' said Cassius. But in the fourth round, Henry punched Cassius hard and knocked him down.

'My people felt that punch in Africa,' Cassius said later.

Luckily for Cassius, it was near the end of the fourth round and he had time in his corner to rest. In the fifth round, however, Cassius cut Cooper's eye very badly, and he had to retire. Cassius was right; Cooper went in five rounds.

Angelo Dundee was very excited about his young fighter. 'You're ready for Sonny Liston,' he said after the Cooper fight. 'You're ready to fight the World Champion.'

* A jive was an informal word for a joke.

CHAPTER 3
'I am the greatest!'

Sonny Liston was the World Heavyweight Champion.
Unlike Cassius Clay, Liston had a hard life as a child in
St. Louis, Missouri. He was one of thirteen children and
his father often hit him. He tried to go to school when
he was thirteen years old. Everyone laughed because
he couldn't read, so he left. He got a gun and was often
in trouble with the police. At just twenty, Liston was in
prison. But prison was good for him, because he learned
how to box there. He became a hard fighter. 'Nobody can
defeat Liston,' the sports writers said.

Was Cassius Clay ready to fight the hard man of
boxing? Cassius was a boy when he won the Olympics
in 1960; after more than three years of hard work, he was
now a man. He was twenty-one years old, and had fifteen
fights behind him. If nobody could defeat Liston, nobody
could defeat Cassius either, said Angelo. But when news
of the fight between Clay and Liston at Miami Beach came
out, the boxing world laughed.

'This is the end for the pretty boy with the big mouth,'
they said.

A few months before the fight, Cassius appeared on
the front of *Time* magazine. People were very interested
in him and his picture sold newspapers. He was a very
good-looking man with a fine body. *Time* magazine's
sports writer was worried. Liston would hurt this happy
young man full of new ideas.

Sports writers didn't agree about Cassius Clay. The
older ones didn't like him. He wasn't their idea of a boxer.
The younger guys loved him. It was easy to write about
him. He was always saying or doing something funny.

Before his fight with Liston, for example, he said:

'Float like a butterfly, sting like a bee.'*

The 5th Street Gym had some famous visitors before the fight. One day, the Beatles came. They were in Miami for a show, and they wanted a photo with Cassius at the gym. Cassius was happy to take pictures with anyone, and he always said yes. When the Beatles tried to get a picture with Sonny Liston, he sent them away.

The Beatles and Cassius Clay

* This is the most famous thing that Ali said. Can you understand what he meant?

Cassius continued making jokes about Sonny Liston up to the day of the fight. He loved to talk about himself too. He called himself 'the greatest', and the newspapers called him the 'Louisville Lip*'.

'This will be the easiest fight of my life,' said Cassius. 'I'm too fast. He's old. I'm young. He ain't** pretty. I'm pretty.'

The sports writers laughed, but they didn't believe him. The fight was taking place at Miami Beach, and one writer found the quickest road to the hospital.

'Clay will be in the hospital after the fight,' said the writer's boss. 'Get there first!'

As the boxers waited to start, Cassius danced around the ring practising his punches. Deep inside, Cassius didn't believe his own words.

'That's the only time I was ever scared in the ring,' Ali said later. 'Sonny Liston. First time. First round. He says he's gonna kill me.'

There wasn't a big crowd. 'Liston will finish Cassius after one or two rounds,' people said. 'I don't want to see that.'

Cassius was taller than Liston and that helped him. He started well. He danced away from Liston's dangerous punches. Suddenly, at the end of each round, he started punching Liston. He punched hard and fast, and cut Liston above his left eye. Liston's doctor put something on the cut at the end of the round.

Cassius nearly lost in the fifth round. Something got in his eyes, and he couldn't see. Was it something Liston's doctor used on Liston's cut? Maybe.

'I can't fight,' Cassius said.

* lip = 'someone who talks a lot' in informal U.S. English

** ain't = 'isn't' in informal English

'You must fight,' said Angelo Dundee, and washed Cassius's eyes with water. 'Go!'

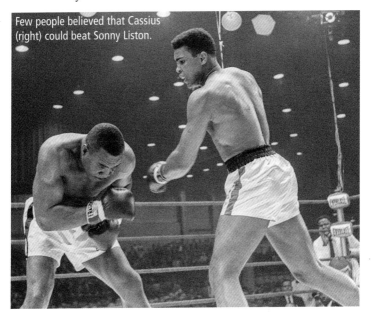

Few people believed that Cassius (right) could beat Sonny Liston.

During the fifth round, Cassius really couldn't see. He moved quickly to escape Liston's punches. He was still standing at the end of the round. Angelo washed his eyes again. In the sixth round, Cassius was back to his best. He punched Liston again and again. He hurt Liston, who was very tired.

At the beginning of the seventh round, Sonny Liston couldn't get out of his corner. He retired.

'I am the greatest,' shouted Cassius to the crowd.

'Eat your words,' shouted Cassius to the sports writers. 'I shook up the world! I'm king of the world.'

On 25th February, 1964, Cassius Clay became Heavyweight Champion of the World. He surprised the world. And he was about to surprise the world again.

CHAPTER 4
Muhammad Ali

'I shook up the world!' shouted Cassius Clay after his win over Sonny Liston. A few weeks later, he shook up the world again. He gave himself a new name and a new religion.

'My name is Muhammad Ali,' he said, 'and I am a Muslim.'

* * *

The Clay family in Louisville were Christians, and Cassius was a Christian when he arrived in Miami. He knew the Bible well, but when he sat in church, it didn't feel right. He looked at the pictures of Jesus Christ on the walls.

'Why does he have blond hair and blue eyes? Why is he white?' asked the young Cassius. 'Where are the black people in this religion?'

All his life, Ali loved to walk around the streets and talk to ordinary people. Soon after he came to Miami in 1960 and before people knew him, he met a man selling a religious newspaper on a street corner. This man was a Muslim, and he was in a group called the Nation of Islam. He had a very different story to tell from the Christian story.

When Cassius went to a Nation of Islam meeting in Miami, he liked what he heard. He liked the idea of a black country, with no white people and no white laws. The teaching answered his questions about being black. And the Nation of Islam welcomed him. At first, he went in secret, through the back door. The boxing world would not like his new religion.

'They'll stop my fight against Liston,' he thought, so he didn't tell them.

Malcolm X (left) was in the Nation of Islam and became a special friend to Ali.

Black groups in the 1960s

There was trouble between white and black people in large parts of the USA in the 1960s. Black African-Americans were second-class throughout the United States, and segregation still existed in the South. Segregation became against the law in 1964, but many white people did not want black people in their world. Black people fought back in different ways.

- Some did nothing and lived in their black areas, like the Clays in Louisville. Many of these black areas were very poor.

- Martin Luther King started the civil rights movement in 1955. Black people must have the same laws as white people, he said. Black people must enjoy the American way of life too. He led thousands of black Americans to Washington, DC. 'I have a dream,' he told them. He dreamed of an America where colour was not important.

Martin Luther King speaks to thousands of followers.

- The Black Panther group wanted big changes. They started later, in 1966. They gave guns to ordinary black people. They asked them to watch the police. They gave free breakfasts to poor black children. Black Panther doctors and dentists helped poor black people for free.

Black Panthers show their feelings.

- The Nation of Islam group started in 1930, and the leader was Elijah Muhammad. This was his message: 'Black people were the first people in the world, but then a very bad man made white people. All white people are bad, and they still think of black people as slaves. White laws are for white people only. When the world ends, Allah* will save black people. White people will die. We are happy to be black, and we are the good people of the world.'

Elijah Muhammad

The Nation of Islam had schools, mosques* and businesses in the cities. They wanted their own Nation (or Country) of Islam, with no white people in it. They were a Muslim group, but they believed very different things from other Muslims.

* Allah is 'God' in Islam; a mosque is like a Muslim 'church'

When he fought Sonny Liston, he was still Cassius Clay. He had a special guest in a ringside seat on the night of the fight. The sports writers saw this man and wrote about him. This man was very unpopular with white America. He was an important man in the Nation of Islam, and his name was Malcolm X. He was Cassius's close friend and teacher.

* * *

After he defeated Sonny Liston, Cassius felt he was ready to fight the world.

'I am joining the Nation of Islam,' he told the newspapers. 'Elijah Muhammad is giving me a new name. Clay is my slave name. I didn't choose it and I don't want it. From today, my name is Muhammad Ali.' When people tried to use his old slave name, he became angry.

The civil rights movement did not like the Nation of Islam or agree with their ideas. But they loved to see this exciting young man turn away from white America. He stood up for black people and he became a black hero. Martin Luther King didn't like Malcolm X, but he wrote to Ali to say, 'Well done!'

* * *

When Ali went to Miami, he liked everyone but he didn't know any young women. He wanted a girlfriend but he didn't know how to find one. Herbert Muhammad, Elijah's son, introduced him to Sonji Roi, who worked in a bar. Herbert thought Ali and Sonji would have a nice evening out, and say goodbye. But Ali fell in love. They got married a few weeks later, in August 1964. Sonji became a Muslim, but she hated the style of clothes that Muslim women wore. She continued to wear make-up and expensive evening dresses. She spent a lot of money on different hairstyles. Ali believed in the family, and wanted his wife to be a good Muslim. He left Sonji and it was over by January 1966.

Ali and Sonji

∗ ∗ ∗

After his win over Liston, Ali travelled to Africa. He travelled on an African plane, and was very surprised to see black pilots flying the plane. When he arrived, big crowds waited to meet him. He felt at home.

'This is what the Nation of Islam wants,' he said. He continued to talk to people about the Nation of Islam, but he always had his own ideas.

'I am happy to welcome white folks into my life,' he said. 'But if white people don't want me in their homes, workplaces or restaurants, then I do not want to be there. I want to show the world that you can be a new kind of black man.'

Many black people and Muslims did not like the Nation of Islam and its ideas, but they loved Ali. They loved his words. Ali didn't hate white people. He didn't hate anyone. But he didn't like black men playing the white man's game. He had a problem with his own sport. 'Boxing is a lot of white men watching two black men hurting each other,' he said. Many black fighters were Christians. He called them names, and upset them.

Before Ali's trip to Africa, Elijah Muhammad asked Malcolm X to leave the Nation of Islam. He did not like Malcolm X's new ideas. Malcolm X went to Mecca*, and he saw white Muslims with blue eyes and blond hair. He saw that they were true Muslims like the black Muslims. He became a different kind of Muslim – a Sunni Muslim. Ali turned his back on his old friend and stayed with the Nation of Islam. The following spring, some men killed Malcolm X. Was Elijah Muhammad behind the killing? Maybe. Did Ali know about it before it happened? Maybe.

∗ ∗ ∗

The boxing world did not like the new Ali. Most sports writers continued to call him Cassius Clay. That autumn, Ali's four years with the Louisville millionaires ended. He chose a new man to look after his business life – Herbert Muhammad, son of Elijah Muhammad. This choice was not popular either.

Ali the man was very kind. He gave his money and his time to anyone who asked for it. He loved people, and he was always smiling. Ali the boxer was not always kind.

* Mecca is a special place for Muslims in Saudi Arabia; all Muslims must visit Mecca once in their life.

Sometimes he wasn't very nice before a fight or in the ring. In 1967 he fought Ernie Terrell. Ernie wanted to upset Ali before the fight. So he called him 'Clay'. Ernie thought it was part of the game. It worked too well. Ali was upset, and very angry too. This was bad news for Ernie. Ali was much too good for him. Every time Ali punched Ernie, he shouted, 'What's my name?'

'Why don't you knock him out?' asked Angelo Dundee, at the end of an early round.

But Ali wanted to hurt Ernie. He punched him for fifteen rounds, and hurt Ernie very badly. Nobody enjoyed the fight, and Ali was sorry about it later.

∗ ∗ ∗

Ali was becoming the greatest fighter in the story of boxing. He had fast hands and fast feet, and he could think fast.

'I didn't train him,' said Angelo, 'I just helped him.'

Ali danced around the ring with his hands down, moving out of the way of punches. Then he punched back, as fast as lightning. But the secret of his great boxing was hard work. Boxers didn't win fights in the ring, Ali knew. They won them in the gym, running on the road, training every day.

'I hate every minute of training,' Ali said. 'But I have to do it. I want to live the rest of my life as a champion.'

In 1966, a boxing crowd of 35,000 watched Ali defeat Cleveland Williams in Houston, Texas. Ali put on a brilliant show, finishing Williams in three rounds. In March the following year, Ali knocked out Zora Folley in New York in the seventh round. Who could defeat him now? He was far ahead of other fighters.

But Ali's next fight was not in the boxing ring.

CHAPTER 5
'I won't fight'

In 1965, the year after Ali became Heavyweight Champion of the World, America joined the Vietnam War. The government sent thousands of men to South East Asia. Soon there were not enough men. Every young man aged 18 to 25 in the United States took tests. Ali took his. In the reading and writing test, he did badly. This meant that he did not have to go to war.

'I said the greatest, not the cleverest,' he joked.

By 1966, the U.S. needed even more men to fight in Vietnam. The government made an easier reading and writing test. Ali took it again. This was around the time that he stopped working with the Louisville millionaires. A letter came for Ali. He had to go to Vietnam to fight in the war. At first, he couldn't understand it.

'Why me?' he asked. 'After each fight, I pay thousands of dollars to the U.S. government. I pay for 50,000 fighting men.'

Ali tells people he won't fight in the war in Vietnam.

Then he thought about it. He talked to Elijah Muhammad. He felt he couldn't fight in Vietnam. His religion did not allow him to fight.

'I have no fight with the Vietcong*,' he said. 'Why are they asking me to go 10,000 miles* from home and kill brown people while black people in Louisville have to live like dogs?'

Ali's words were on the front page of newspapers around the world. The newspapers in the U.S. were angry. In April 1967, Ali told the government, 'I won't fight.' Less than one hour later, Ali's boxing life was over.

'We're taking your boxing titles and we will not allow you to fight again in the United States,' said the head of U.S. boxing.

'You cannot leave the United States. You will go to prison for five years. You will pay $10,000,' said the U.S. government.

Ali did not fight again until 1970. The best years in a boxer's life are ages twenty-five to twenty-eight. Those are the years that Ali lost. 'They took his best years,' said Angelo Dundee. 'You don't get a long time to fight as a boxer.'

He did not go to prison. The government allowed Ali to appeal. But he had to wait more than three years for his appeal. While he waited, he could not fight in America. He could not fight in another country because he could not leave the United States. Ali paid a very high price for his ideas.

In those three years, many Americans came to agree with Ali about the Vietnam War. But that did not help Ali.

∗ ∗ ∗

* His famous actual words: 'I ain't got nothing against them Vietcong.'; 1 mile = 1.6 kilometres

THE VIETNAM

WHY WAS THERE A WAR?

In 1954, Vietnam became two countries. Communists ran North Vietnam, and their leader was Ho Chi Minh. The leader in the South was Ngo Dinh Diem, a friend of America. The U.S. government sent guns to the South, and helped to train Diem's men. But Diem was a hard man, and many people in the South did not want him as leader. They wanted to join the Communist North. They formed small fighting groups, and they were called the Viet Cong.

THE COLD WAR

This was the time of the Cold War, which followed the end of World War II in 1945. The United States led Western countries, calling themselves the 'free world'. The Soviet Union led Communist countries, with China behind them.

'If one country in South East Asia becomes Communist,' said the United States, 'they all become Communist.'

THE COST OF WAR

From 1965 to 1973, the United States took part in the Vietnam War. The Vietnamese called this the American War. During this time, around 250,000 South Vietnamese men and 58,200 American men died fighting.

'LET'S GET OUT OF VIETNAM'

It was a terrible war. The U.S. government tried to say they were winning. But photographs and films from Vietnam told a different story. At first, most American people believed in the war.

WAR

But over the years, the news from Vietnam changed that. In one week in June 1969, for example, 241 Americans died in Vietnam. On 27th June, 1969, *Life* magazine had photographs of all 241 men. By now, most Americans wanted to be out of the war.

WHAT WAS IT FOR?

President Nixon brought home 500,000 American men in 1970. The war was over in 1973, with North and South Vietnam agreeing to live together. That lasted for two years. In 1975, Ho Chi Minh and the Communist North took over the whole country. Many people thought that the war was for nothing.

In 1967 Ali married his second wife, Belinda Boyd. Belinda joined the Nation of Islam and became Khalilah Ali. Most people still called her Belinda. They had four children.

Belinda and Ali worked together through a difficult time. He started to give talks at universities around the country. They wrote his words together, and Ali learned them. He talked about being black in a white world. He talked about not going to Vietnam. It gave Ali time to think about his ideas. He was happy with a microphone, and loved speaking to a crowd. The students asked him questions about his religious ideas. 'I'm only a boxer,' he said, 'but people ask me questions like I'm in the government.' His talks usually ended with all the students shouting, 'You are the greatest!'

A television man called Howard Cosell helped Ali too. He often invited Ali onto his TV show, and gave him work on TV boxing programmes. Ali even appeared in a musical show on Broadway* called *Buck White*. But he wanted to box. Black friends in government tried to find places for him to fight, but every door was closed.

* New York's theatre street

CHAPTER 6
The 'Rumble in the Jungle*'

As the American people turned against the Vietnam War, Ali's friends were finally able to get him a fight. Ali was still waiting for the law to decide on his appeal. In October 1970, Ali fought Jerry Quarry in Atlanta, Georgia, his first fight for over three years. The fight was over by the third round, and Ali was the winner. But he was not the same fighter, and everyone could see that he was much slower. Many famous black people were there to welcome back their hero. The singer Diana Ross, the religious leader Jesse Jackson and Coretta Scott King, wife of Martin Luther King, were in seats next to the ring.

It wasn't Jerry Quarry that Ali wanted to fight. It was Joe Frazier, who had Ali's title as Heavyweight Champion of the World. But was it the best time for Ali to fight Smokin' Joe?

Joe Frazier had a hard life as a child, like Sonny Liston. His parents were kind, unlike Liston's father. The large family lived in the country, and the white bosses were not kind to their black workers. Joe practised boxing every day in the back garden. He worked for two local white men, but then he got in trouble with them. They were wrong, but Joe had to leave. At fifteen, he went out into the world alone. He decided to become a boxer. In 1964 he became Olympic champion and in 1970, he was Heavyweight Champion of the World. Joe was a good friend to Ali during Ali's three years away from boxing. He thought it was wrong to take Ali's titles away. It was wrong to stop him boxing. Ali wasn't always a good friend to Joe.

* rumble = fight; jungle = very hot place with lots of trees and animals

35

The fight took place at Madison Square Garden in New York City on 8th March 1971. Ali wasn't ready. He wasn't quick or strong enough, but he wanted his title back. The fight was close and hard. After fourteen rounds, the winner wasn't clear. Then, in Round 15, Frazier punched Ali's jaw and broke it. Ali fell onto his back. The crowd couldn't believe it when Ali stood up and started to fight back. Ali lost the match, but he won the love of the boxing world. He was a hero. After three years away, he nearly

Smokin' Joe broke Ali's jaw in New York City.

won his title from the world's best boxer at the time. Ali still believed in himself. He knew he was cleverer than any other boxer. He just had to find a new way to win.

Six weeks later, Ali learned the result of his appeal. He won. He did not have to go to prison. He could fight again. He could win his title back again.

But how could he fight again? He wasn't fast now and he couldn't dance away from his opponents. He wasn't quick and he couldn't surprise his opponents. He studied

his fight with Joe Frazier, and he found the answer. His opponent could punch him. He would lie against the ropes and keep his head back. The other fighter could punch his arms and body, but would then become tired. At that moment, Ali could jump forward and start punching.

This new style was good news for his boxing. He could win fights again. It was very bad news for his body. He paid a high price later in his life.

Over the next three years, Ali defeated ten opponents, including George Chuvalo, Jerry Quarry, Floyd Patterson and Joe Bugner.

'I can defeat anyone,' he believed, and he stopped training hard.

In March 1973, he lost to Ken Norton. Norton broke Ali's jaw in Round 2. Ali continued to fight to the end, but lost. It took six months for his jaw to get better. Then he fought Norton again. There was no mistake this time, and he won. When he fought Joe Frazier again in 1974, Ali won. People everywhere followed every move that Ali made. He was one of the most famous men in the world.

Around this time, Ali made one of his many visits to London. He came often, to sell his books, to see his friends and to appear on TV shows. He fought more fights in London than in any other country outside America. A school teacher stopped Ali outside his expensive London hotel in 1974. The teacher's name was Paul Stephenson, and he was also a leader of Britain's civil rights movement. He worked at a school in a poor area of south London.

'Can you come to my school?' Paul asked. 'It would bring hope into the children's lives.'

Ali at Tulse Hill school, London.

'I'm a very busy man,' said Ali. 'How much can you pay me?'

'I don't have any money,' said Paul.

Ali laughed and went with Paul to his school in Tulse Hill. A thousand children waited in the school hall. They didn't know what was happening. It was very quiet.

Then Ali appeared. All the children jumped up. It was very noisy.

Ali practised his boxing moves with some of the children. He spoke to them and asked them questions. He wanted to bring hope into their lives. He wanted to be a different kind of superstar.

'You can walk up to me and say hello without paying,' he often said. 'I am the People's Champion.'

He loved to spend time with ordinary people. On the same visit, Ali was signing his new book in a central London bookshop. The news travelled quickly, and a huge crowd of people was soon outside. Cars and buses couldn't move along the street for hours.

∗ ∗ ∗

In 1973, George Foreman took the World Heavyweight boxing title from Joe Frazier in Jamaica. Ali was waiting for the winner. George and Ali were both American, but they decided not to fight in the United States. They took their match to Africa, fighting in Kinshasa in Zaire*. The newspapers called the fight the 'Rumble in the Jungle'. Ali loved being in Africa and looking out from the ring at the black crowd.

The fight had everything. It was in an exciting place. There was a lot of money for the two fighters – five million dollars each. And either man could win.

George Foreman was a strong, young fighter with a very big punch. Ali, now thirty-two, was seven years older. It was a very hot night in Kinshasa. Ali followed his plan. For seven rounds, he allowed Foreman to punch him. Ali lay against the ropes and took George's punches on his body. In Round 8, Ali came off the ropes and said quietly in Foreman's ear, 'Can't you hit me harder than that, George?' Ali then punched Foreman lightly with his left glove, and hit him hard with his right. He knocked Foreman to the floor and won the fight. Ali was Heavyweight Champion of the World again.

Ali ran to the sports writers next to the ring.

'What did I tell you?' he shouted. 'What did I tell you?'

For the first time, a U.S. President invited Ali to the White House after the 'Rumble in the Jungle'. It was December 1974, and President Gerald Ford wanted to meet America's great fighter.

'Why did you let me come?' he asked President Ford. 'Now I want your job.'

This was the moment for Ali to end his boxing life. His family, his manager and his doctor all said the same thing: 'Why don't you retire? You're the greatest.'

But Ali couldn't stop.

* Zaire is now the Democratic Republic of Congo

CHAPTER 7
On the ropes

In 1975, Elijah Muhammad, leader of the Nation of Islam, died. One of Elijah's sons became leader. He changed many of the Nation of Islam ideas. Ali agreed with these changes, but he decided to become a Sunni Muslim the same year. He left the Nation of Islam.

✳ ✳ ✳

Ali made it difficult for himself as he got ready to fight Joe Frazier for a third and final time. For this fight they went to Manila, in the Philippines. It was 1975.

First, Ali gave Smokin' Joe a new name – 'gorilla'. He probably chose it so he could say, 'I'm going to fight the gorilla in Manila.' But it's a very bad name to give to a black man. Joe was very upset.

'I like my opponent to be angry,' Ali told sports writer Dick Schaap, 'then he can't think.'

Next, Ali brought his new girlfriend to Manila. Her name was Veronica Porsche. He was still married to Belinda, but he took Veronica to meet the President of the Philippines in Manila.

'Meet my wife, Veronica,' Ali said to President Marcos.

Back home in America, Belinda was watching on TV. She took the next plane to Manila. Ali and Belinda spent the night before the fight shouting at each other.

The fight took place at 10 o'clock in the morning Manila time, so that people around the world could watch it on television. That meant it was terribly hot, as hot as 49°C in the ring. Ali continued to upset Joe in the ring.

'You don't have it, Joe, you don't have it!' he said.

'We'll see,' said Joe.

Ali took his girlfriend Veronica Porsche (centre, behind Ali) to meet President Marcos of the Philippines

Ali won the first two rounds with his quick feet and fast hands. In Round 3, Ali lay against the ropes. Joe hit him many times, and by the fifth round, Joe was winning. Ali couldn't stop his punches. Ali took two big hits from Joe in the sixth round, but Ali stayed on his feet.

'I thought Joe Frazier was finished,' said Ali at the start of the seventh.

'You thought wrong,' answered Joe.

By now, both men were really tired.

'Man, this is the closest I've ever been to dying,' said Ali to Angelo Dundee. By now, Frazier couldn't see well. In the fourteenth round Ali hit Frazier with thirty big punches.

'I can't fight anymore,' said Ali to Angelo. He was ready to retire. Seconds later, Frazier retired. Ali had won.

Neither man enjoyed the fight. Before the fight, Frazier thought they were friends until Ali called him 'gorilla'. Years later, Joe's son met Ali.

'My father was upset,' said Joe's son. 'Why did you call

him "gorilla"?'

Ali cried when he heard this. He said sorry to Joe and the Frazier family. The two fighters met when they were older. Ali couldn't speak by then, but he and Joe held hands.

Belinda left Ali after the Manila fight, and in June 1977, Ali and Veronica were married. They already had one daughter, and their second daughter arrived in December. They stayed married until 1986, when Veronica left Ali. He was seeing other women.

Ali still didn't retire from the ring. He lost his Heavyweight title to Leon Spinks in 1978 in Las Vegas.

Ali with daughters Hana and Laila.

Spinks was eleven years younger than Ali, who was getting too old to box. 'Enough,' said his doctor Ferdie Pacheco. Ali refused. He wanted that title back again.

Eight months later he fought Spinks again, this time in New Orleans. Millions watched on TV. Nobody could believe it when Ali won, and became Heavyweight Champion for the third time at the age of thirty-six.

Ali continued to box until he was nearly forty. Already there were signs that he was ill. He couldn't speak clearly. He couldn't move fast. He was always tired and he couldn't stop his hands shaking.

In 1984, his doctor told him the bad news. Ali had Parkinson's Disease. If you have this, your arms and legs shake, you move slowly and you become very tired. You also find it very hard to speak, and that was the worst news for Ali.

MUHAMMAD ALI: Champion of the World

Professional boxing life: 21 years

Time lost: 3.5 years waiting for his appeal, when the U.S. government did not allow him to fight

Number of fights: 61

Total number of wins: 56, including 37 knock-outs

Number of wins without losing: 31, until Joe Frazier defeated him in 1971

Olympic title: 1

World Heavyweight titles: 3, more than any other boxer

Money from boxing: $60m/£37.2m

CHAPTER 8
Greatest of All Time, Inc.

Back when Ali was in his twenties, he often returned to Louisville to visit his mother. His parents lived on Verona Way, in the house that Ali bought for them. Ali always played with the local children. On one visit, he met six-year-old Lonnie Williams. Her family lived opposite the Clays in Verona Way, and her mother and Ali's mother were good friends. Ali and Lonnie became good friends too.

Ali talks to local children outside his mother's house in Verona Way, Louisville. The little girl is six-year-old Lonnie Williams.

In 1982 Ali invited Lonnie to lunch in Louisville. She was worried when she saw him. He seemed unhappy and unwell. She talked to Ali's wife Veronica. Lonnie offered to move to Los Angeles to look after Ali. Veronica agreed; she and Ali were not living together.

Lonnie went to university in Los Angeles. She wanted to complete her business studies course. When Lonnie was twenty-nine and Ali was forty-four, they were married in Louisville. Lonnie had become a Muslim, and this was about the time Ali learned he had Parkinson's Disease.

Lonnie now used her business studies. She built a business called the Greatest of All Time, Inc. (GOAT, Inc.) to look after Ali's money and his name. Ali finally agreed to retire, and he and Lonnie went to live at Berrien Springs, Michigan. He woke up at five o'clock every morning to study the Qu'ran*. 'I didn't truly understand Islam until 1983,' he said.

Ali was very free with his money and time, and a lot of his money disappeared into the pockets of his 'friends'. To get some money in the bank again, Ali had to try new things. Businesses offered him money for his name and face. He was the first boxer to appear on boxes of Wheaties on people's breakfast tables.

In 2005, Lonnie and Ali had enough money to open the Muhammad Ali Center in Louisville. It helps bring hope and understanding to people everywhere. 'Be Great; Do Great Things,' says the sign on the outside.

Parkinson's Disease didn't stop Ali from travelling around the world. He used his famous name to help the poor. He went to Liberia in West Africa with food and clothing for people with nothing. He went to Cuba to visit local hospitals.

* The Qu'ran is the book of Islam.

Ali loved his visit to Cuba, where he visited children's hospitals.

In 1990, when America was fighting Iraq, he went to Baghdad to see Saddam Hussein, the President of Iraq. Saddam had fifteen American prisoners, and the United States wanted them back. Ali waited five days to see Saddam. Ali spent the time in Baghdad, talking to ordinary Iraqis and visiting schools and mosques. Finally, Saddam saw Ali. He gave him the fifteen prisoners. The men were very happy to get home. 'He's our guy,' they said of Ali.

The Olympic Games of 1996 took place in Atlanta, Georgia. As millions of people watched on the opening night, Ali appeared. He couldn't smile anymore. His hand was shaking as he lit the Olympic fire. Many people cried when they saw him. They were crying because they loved him, and because he showed the world the real America.

He appeared again at the London Olympic Games of 2012. Lonnie helped him walk a few steps. By now, he was very ill. He died four years later in 2016.

Ali at the Olympic Games,
Atlanta, 1996

EPILOGUE

Muhammad Ali died on 3rd June, 2016 in hospital in
Phoenix, Arizona. He was seventy-four years old. His
family took his body back to his hometown of Louisville.
As the car carrying Ali drove along Muhammad Ali
Boulevard, the crowds threw flowers and shouted, 'Ali!
Ali!'

'He decided very young to write his own story,' said,
Bill Clinton, ex-President of the United States.

'Muhammad Ali was the greatest show in the world,'
said George Foreman, an opponent.

'Muhammad wants young people to learn from his
life. When times are hard, learn to be strong – that's his
message,' said Lonnie Ali, his wife.

'Muhammad Ali was America,' said Barack Obama, the
President. 'What a man!'

THE SPORT

Boxing is a simple sport. Two people fight until one person can't fight any more. Thousands of years ago, the Greeks and Romans loved boxing matches. In those times, boxers often killed their opponents. Boxing today is safer, but there are still dangers.

The match

Today, a men's boxing match has 12 rounds. Each round is two to three minutes long, with one minute between rounds.

The Queensberry rules

In 1867, the Marquess of Queensberry wrote down some rules for boxing in London. These are some of them:

- You can't punch below your opponent's belt – their middle.

- You can't punch your opponent when they are on the floor.

- You can't hit with your head, feet, elbows or the inside of your hands.

The dangers

Boxing was not safe for Ali. He loved boxing, but it killed him in the end. 'Hard punches to the head gave Ali Parkinson's Disease,' said his doctor.

'Boxing hurts your brain,' says Irish boxer Barry McGuigan. Doctors agree. When boxers get older, they often forget things. They move more slowly. They can become very unhappy. And their personality can change.

English idiom from boxing

"That was below the belt." = That was a horrible and unfair thing to say or do.

OF BOXING

Women's boxing

'It's a horrible idea!' said a sports reporter in 1948. He was talking about women's boxing. The sport was against the law in Britain until 1998, but then people changed their ideas.

At the 2012 Olympics in London, women boxed for the first time. The crowds loved it! British boxer Nicola Adams became the first woman ever to win an Olympic gold medal for boxing. She won gold again at the Rio Olympics in 2016.

Nicola Adams at the Olympics 2016

Only one of Muhammad Ali's nine children became a boxer – Laila Ali. Like her dad, she was a very successful boxer. She fought 24 times, and she won all 24 fights. One of her fights was against Jackie Frazier, daughter of Joe Frazier. Laila retired in 2007 as Super Middleweight Champion of the World.

Boxing is the only sport where you try to hurt another person. Is it too dangerous?

In numbers

★ In Britain, **20%** of people taking part in boxing are women.

★ Women's boxing takes place in **120** countries.

★ There are more than **500,000** women boxers around the world.

What do these words mean? You can use a dictionary.

belt brain elbow personality rule simple successful

PROLOGUE–CHAPTER 2

Before you read

You can use your dictionary.

1 Match the person to the description.

champion   hero   leader   opponent   slave   trainer

a) *This person* tells you how to play your sport better.

b) You try to beat *this person* in a sports match.

c) *This person* wins first prize in a competition.

d) *This person* is the top person in a country.

e) *This person* works for another person for free and cannot leave.

f) Everyone thinks *this person* has done brilliant things.

2 Choose the correct option in bold to complete these sentences.

a) If you do something wrong and the police catch you, you go to **the gym / prison**.

b) Many people pay to join a **prison / gym** and never go there!

c) The champion wore her **medal / title** all day long.

d) The same two football teams win the **medal / title** every year - it's boring.

e) The **lightning / crowd** was loud and lit the night sky - I was frightened.

f) The **lightning / crowd** was loud and angry - I was frightened.

g) The car left the road and **knocked down / cut** a tree.

h) The car window broke, and the driver **knocked down / cut** his hand.

3 Put the correct word in each space.

defeated   government   law   local   punch   style   retire

a) The .... decided to introduce a new .... to stop people driving and texting at the same time.

b) The .... people welcomed the new family into their village.

c) The girl danced with brilliant .... and won first prize.

d) The .... was loud and hard, and everyone in the crowd turned away.

e) Life can seem empty when you .... from work.

f) Manchester City .... Chelsea to win the game three-one.

4 What do you know about Muhammad Ali? Think of three things.

After you read

5 Answer these questions.
  a) What did someone take from Cassius when he was 12?
  b) Which part of town was not safe for Cassius and Rudolph?
  c) Why did white people make the 'Jim Crow laws'?
  d) Why did the husband and brother of a white woman kill Emmet Till?
  e) Which two cities did Cassius visit in the summer of 1960?
  f) What kind of welcome did Cassius get back in Louisville after the Olympics?

6 Correct the mistakes.
  a) In his first fight for his new Louisville team, Cassius beat Sugar Ray Robinson.
  b) Cassius didn't enjoy his new life in Miami.
  c) He learned a new way of moving and punching in Cuba.
  d) He was more interested in being famous than in training hard.
  e) Henry Cooper knocked Cassius down and beat him.

7 *Time* magazine wanted Cassius on the front of their magazine before he beat Sonny Liston. Why were people so interested in him, do you think?

CHAPTERS 3–4

Before you read

8 Choose the correct meaning for these words.
  a) Your **religion** is …
  ❏ the ideas you believe about god or gods.
  ❏ the things you remember.

  b) If you **shake** people **up**, they are …
  ❏ surprised.
  ❏ angry.

After you read

9 Answer the questions.
   a) What did Sonny Liston learn in prison?
   b) Why did the newspapers call Cassius the 'Louisville Lip'?
   c) How did Cassius really feel when he faced Liston in the ring?
   d) What problem did Cassius have in Round 5?
   e) What title did Cassius win in February 1964?

10 Are these sentences true or false?
   a) After beating Sonny Liston, Cassius Clay became Muhammad Ali.
   b) He felt the Christian religion was for white people.
   c) As soon as he heard the ideas of the Nation of Islam, he started going openly to the meetings.
   d) Sonji Ray left Ali in January 1966.
   e) Ali was always nice to his opponents.

11 Ali tried to shake up the world with his ideas about life as well as his boxing. Should sports stars just talk about sport, do you think?

CHAPTERS 5–6

Before you read

12 Match the words and definitions.
   appeal   jaw
   a) If you lose a fight in law, you can usually do this.
   b) This opens so you can eat and speak.

After you read

13 Answer the questions.
   a) Why did Ali have to take the government reading and writing test a second time?
   b) Why wouldn't Ali go to Vietnam?
   c) The head of U.S. boxing and the government were very hard on Ali because of Vietnam. What five things did they do?
   d) How long did Ali's appeal take?
   e) How did Ali make money when he wasn't boxing?

14 Put these events in the correct order.
- **a)** Ali beat ten fighters, including Floyd Patterson and Joe Bugner.
- **b)** Ali got back in the ring after three years and defeated Jerry Quarry.
- **c)** George Foreman lost his Heavyweight title to Ali in Africa.
- **d)** Joe Frazier broke Ali's jaw in New York City.
- **e)** Ken Norton broke Ali's jaw in Round 2.
- **f)** The U.S. President invited Ali to the White House.

15 How did Ali change his fighting style after he came back to boxing in 1970? Was he right to change it, do you think?

CHAPTERS 7–EPILOGUE

Before you read

16 Why didn't Ali retire after the Rumble in the Jungle, do you think?

After you read

17 Answer the questions.
- **a)** Who did Ali upset by calling him a 'gorilla'?
- **b)** Who did Ali take to meet the President of the Philippines?
- **c)** Who won the fight in Manila?
- **d)** Who left Ali after the fight in Manila?
- **e)** Who told Ali to retire?
- **f)** Who did Ali defeat to become Heavyweight Champion for the third time?

18 Are these sentences true or false?
- **a)** As a child, Ali's fourth wife, Lonnie, lived opposite Ali's parents on Verona Way in Louisville.
- **b)** Ali was fifteen years younger than Lonnie.
- **c)** Lonnie looked after Ali and his money.
- **d)** After he retired, Ali became a Christian again.
- **e)** Ali wasn't able to travel because of his Parkinson's Disease.
- **f)** Ali was the star of the opening night of the 1996 Olympic Games in Atlanta.

NEW WORDS

What do these words mean?

appeal (n & v) ....

champion (n) .... /

      Heavyweight Champion (adj + n) ....

crowd (n) ....

cut (n & v) ....

defeat (n & v) ....

government (n) ....

gym (n) ....

hero (n) ....

jaw (n) ....

knock down (v) .... / knock out (v) ....

      knock-out (n) ....

law (n) ....

lead (v) (past led) .... / leader (n) ....

lightning (n) ....

local (adj) ....

medal (n) .... / gold medal (n) ....

opponent (n) ....

prison (n) ....

punch (n & v) ....

religion (n) .... / religious (adj) ....

retire (v) ....

shake up (v) ....

slave (n) .... / slavery (n) ....

style (n) ....

title (n) ....

train (v) .... / trainer (n) ....